Our Favorite
Freezer-Friendly Recipes

Copyright 2021, Gooseberry Patch
Previously published under ISBN 978-1-93628-374-3

Cover: Homesteader's Casserole (page 65)

Freezer-Friendly Pointers

❋ Spend a day making double batches of favorite foods to freeze...your freezer will be full in no time!

❋ Cool down hot foods before wrapping and freezing. Let just-baked casseroles stand at room temperature for 30 minutes, then chill in the fridge for 30 minutes more. Large pots of simmering soup cool quickly when set in a sink full of ice water.

❋ Pack cooked foods in plastic freezer bags or food containers, or double-wrap tightly in plastic freezer wrap or aluminum foil.

* Label and date packages. You'll find a handy label to copy & cut out on page 24 of this book.

* Most home-cooked foods are tastiest if kept frozen no longer than two to three months. As long as they're frozen solid, though, they don't become harmful to eat.

* Thaw frozen foods in the fridge overnight. If no baking instructions are given, cover casseroles loosely with aluminum foil and bake at 350 degrees for 25 minutes. Uncover and bake 20 to 30 minutes longer, until hot in the center.

* When reheating thawed soup or sauce on the stovetop, make sure it's at a full boil for one minute.

Make your own smoothies. Fill your blender with your favorite frozen fruit. Add juice, milk, yogurt or even ice cream to taste. Garnish with a sprig of mint. Yum!

4

Light & Fluffy Pancakes

Makes 6 to 8 servings

1 c. all-purpose flour
2 T. sugar
2 t. baking powder
1/2 t. salt

1 egg, beaten
1 c. milk
2 T. oil

Stir together flour, sugar, baking powder and salt. Add egg, milk and oil all at once to flour mixture, stirring until blended but still slightly lumpy. Pour batter onto a hot, lightly greased griddle or heavy skillet, about 1/4 cup each for regular pancakes or one tablespoon for silver dollar pancakes. Cook on both sides until golden, turning when surface is bubbly and edges are slightly dry.

Freeze & Serve Instructions: Cool; store in freezer bags. To serve, place frozen pancakes in a single layer on a baking sheet. Cover with aluminum foil; bake at 350 degrees for about 10 minutes.

Use any favorite quiche recipe to make mini quiche appetizers.
Just pour ingredients into greased mini muffin cups and
bake until the centers are set...so simple!

Pepperoni & Cheese Quiche

Serves 4

1 egg, beaten
3/4 c. all-purpose flour
1 c. milk
1/2 t. dried oregano
1/2 t. salt

1/8 t. pepper
1/2 c. Muenster cheese, shredded
1/2 c. shredded Cheddar cheese
1/4 c. pepperoni, finely chopped

Whisk together first 6 ingredients. Stir in cheeses and pepperoni. Pour into an ungreased 8" pie plate; bake at 375 degrees for 30 minutes, or until puffy and golden.

Freeze & Serve Instructions: Bake as directed; cool, wrap and freeze whole or sliced. To serve, thaw in refrigerator for several hours to overnight. Bake at 350 degrees for a few minutes, until warmed through.

Make a quick & easy crumb crust. Spread 2-1/2 tablespoons softened butter in a pie plate, then press 2-1/2 cups cracker crumbs into the butter. Freeze until firm, pour in filling and bake as directed.

Quick & Easy Quiche

Makes 4 to 6 servings

1/2 of a 2.8-oz. pkg. cooked
   bacon
9-inch pie crust
2 8-oz. containers egg substitute

8-oz. jar creamy blue cheese
   salad dressing

Crumble bacon into pie crust. Blend together egg substitute and salad dressing in a large bowl; pour into pie crust. Bake at 350 degrees for 25 to 30 minutes, or until puffed and a knife inserted in the center comes out clean. Cool on a wire rack for 5 minutes before cutting.

Freeze & Serve Instructions: Bake as directed; cool, wrap and freeze whole or sliced. To serve, thaw in refrigerator for several hours to overnight. Bake at 350 degrees for a few minutes, until warmed through.

A retro-style ice cream scoop with a lever is just right for filling muffin cups with batter.

Caramel Apple Muffins

Makes one dozen

2 c. all-purpose flour
3/4 c. sugar
2 t. baking powder
1/2 t. salt
2-1/2 t. cinnamon
1 egg, beaten
1 c. milk

1/4 c. butter, melted
1-1/2 t. vanilla extract
1/2 c. apple, peeled, cored and
    finely diced
12 caramels, unwrapped and
    diced

Combine flour, sugar, baking powder, salt and cinnamon in a large bowl; set aside. In a separate large bowl, mix together egg, milk, butter and vanilla; add flour mixture, stirring just until blended. Stir in apples and caramels. Divide batter evenly among 12 greased muffin cups. Bake at 350 degrees for 25 minutes, or until tops spring back when lightly pressed. Serve warm.

Freeze & Serve Instructions: Cool; place in a freezer bag and freeze. To serve, wrap frozen muffins in heavy aluminum foil and bake at 300 degrees for 12 to 15 minutes.

A loaf of a favorite bread is such a thoughtful
gift...why not include the recipe along with a
pretty vintage towel tied with a bow?

Sunrise Cinnamon Loaves

Makes 2 loaves

18-1/2 oz. pkg. yellow cake mix
   with pudding
4 eggs
3/4 c. oil

3/4 c. water
1 t. vanilla extract
1/2 c. sugar
3 T. cinnamon

Combine first 5 ingredients; beat with an electric mixer on high speed for 3 minutes. Pour into 2 greased and floured 8"x4" loaf pans; set aside. Combine sugar and cinnamon in a small bowl; sprinkle evenly over batter. Spread remaining batter evenly into loaf pans; sprinkle loaves with remaining sugar mixture. Use a knife to gently swirl sugar and cinnamon into batter. Bake at 350 degrees for 45 minutes. Cool on wire racks.

Freeze & Serve Instructions: Place cooled loaves in freezer bags; freeze. To serve, thaw at room temperature or pop a frozen slice or 2 into the toaster.

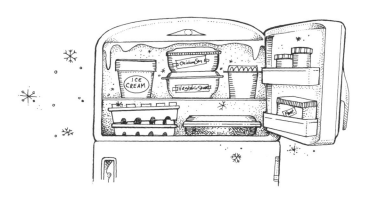

Pack cooked foods in plastic freezer bags or food containers,
or double-wrap tightly in plastic freezer wrap or aluminum foil.
Label and date packages.

Swiss & Rye Bites

8 slices bacon, crisply cooked and crumbled
2.8-oz. can French fried onions, crushed
1/2 c. mayonnaise
3 c. shredded Swiss cheese
14-oz. jar pizza sauce
1 loaf sliced party rye bread

Combine bacon, onions, mayonnaise and cheese in a large bowl. Spread one teaspoon pizza sauce on each slice of bread; top with one tablespoon onion mixture. Arrange on an ungreased baking sheet. Bake at 350 degrees for 12 to 14 minutes, until heated through and cheese is melted.

Freeze & Serve Instructions: Freeze unbaked slices on a baking sheet; store in freezer bags. To serve, place frozen slices on a baking sheet. Bake as directed.

Cheese tends to turn crumbly when frozen...not so good
for a recipe using fresh cheese, but great for casserole
dishes. Stock up when cheese is on sale... just thaw overnight
in the fridge before using.

Italian Cheese Bites

Makes 7 dozen

1 c. butter, softened
8-oz. pkg. shredded
   Italian-blend cheese
1 t. Italian seasoning

1/2 t. dried basil
1/2 t. salt
1/4 t. cayenne pepper
2 c. all-purpose flour

Beat butter with an electric mixer on medium speed until creamy. Add cheese and seasonings; beat until blended. Gradually add flour, stirring just until combined. Cover dough and chill for 2 hours. Form dough into four, 6-inch logs. Cover and chill for an additional hour to overnight. Slice logs 1/4-inch thick. Place slices on parchment paper-lined baking sheets. Bake at 350 degrees for 10 minutes, or until lightly golden. Remove to wire racks to cool. Store in an airtight container for up to 3 days.

Freeze & Serve Instructions: Bake as directed; cool. Freeze slices on a baking sheet; store in freezer bags. To serve, place frozen slices on a baking sheet. Bake at 325 degrees for several minutes, until hot.

Get together with a girlfriend or two and spend a day
making double batches of favorite casseroles to freeze.
Your freezers will be full in no time!

Ham & Cheese Pinwheels

Makes 16 servings

16-oz. pkg. hot roll mix
1/4 c. butter, softened
1-oz. pkg. ranch salad
   dressing mix

1 c. shredded Cheddar cheese
1/2 lb. thinly sliced deli ham

Prepare hot roll mix according to package directions; knead dough
10 times on a well-floured surface. Roll into an 18-inch by 12-inch
rectangle; set aside. Mix butter and dressing mix; spread on dough.
Sprinkle with cheese; arrange ham slices over cheese. Starting at long
edge of dough, roll up jelly-roll style. Pinch raw edges together; place
seam-side down on a greased baking sheet. Pinch ends together. Snip
top of dough at 2-inch intervals. Cover and let rise until double in bulk,
45 minutes to one hour. Bake at 325 degrees for 40 to 50 minutes, until
golden. Slice to serve.

Freeze & Serve Instructions: Bake and slice as directed; cool. Freeze
slices on a baking sheet; store in freezer bags. To serve, return frozen
slices to baking sheet. Bake at 325 degrees for several minutes, until hot.

It's easy to save leftover fresh herbs. Spoon chopped herbs into an ice cube tray, one tablespoon per cube. Cover with water and freeze. Frozen cubes can be dropped right into hot stew or soup.

Parsley-Bacon Sandwich

Makes 10 dozen

1 lb. bacon, crisply cooked
   and crumbled
2 bunches fresh parsley, chopped
1/4 c. mayonnaise
1 t. Worcestershire sauce

1/4 t. garlic powder
1/2 c. butter, softened
1 loaf sandwich bread,
   crust trimmed

Combine bacon, parsley, mayonnaise and Worcestershire sauce to spreading consistency. Mix garlic powder with softened butter. Flatten bread slices with a rolling pin. Spread bread with garlic mixture. Spread parsley mixture over garlic mixture. Roll up slices; wrap in wax paper and twist ends. Chill. To serve, unwrap and slice 5 per roll.

Freeze & Serve Instructions: Freeze unsliced rolls. To serve, unwrap and slice as directed. Thaw at room temperature.

Start a cooking club with friends! Decide on dishes ahead of time, then everyone shops for just a part of the meal. Get together to cook and pack dishes in freezer containers.

22

Broiled Cheese Rounds

Makes 2-1/2 dozen

1 lb. bacon, crisply cooked and
    crumbled
1 lb. shredded sharp Cheddar
    cheese

1 onion, minced
1 to 2 T. mayonnaise
2 loaves sliced party rye bread

In a bowl, combine bacon, cheese and onion; blend in mayonnaise.
Spread mixture onto bread slices; place on an ungreased baking sheet.
Broil 3 to 4 inches from heat source for 3 minutes, until hot and bubbly.

Freeze & Serve Instructions: Freeze unbaked slices on a baking sheet;
store in freezer bags. To serve, place frozen slices on a broiler pan. Broil
3 to 4 inches from heat source until hot and bubbly, about 3 minutes.

Contents: _____

Serves: _____

Prepared on: _____

Enjoy by: _____

Cooking Instructions: _____

_____

_____

_____

_____

_____

© Gooseberry Patch

Copy & cut this handy label to ensure freezer-fresh foods.

Pam's Spinach Squares

Makes 3 to 4 dozen

1 c. all-purpose flour
1 t. salt
1 t. baking powder
2 eggs, beaten
1 c. milk
1/2 c. butter, melted

10-oz. pkg. frozen chopped
    spinach, thawed and drained
1 lb. shredded sharp Cheddar
    cheese
1 onion, chopped

Combine flour, salt and baking powder. Add eggs, milk and butter; stir. Add remaining ingredients and pour into a lightly greased 13"x9" baking pan. Bake at 350 degrees for 35 minutes, or until bubbly around edges. Cut into squares and serve warm.

Freeze & Serve Instructions: Bake as directed; cut into squares and freeze on a baking sheet. Store in freezer bags. To serve, place frozen squares on a baking sheet. Bake at 350 degrees for 20 minutes, until golden.

No crabmeat on hand? Substitute shredded, cooked chicken or even ground turkey for a hearty alternative.

Crab Meltaways

Makes 2 dozen

6-oz. can crabmeat, drained	1 T. mayonnaise
1/2 c. margarine	1/4 t. Worcestershire sauce
5-oz. jar sharp pasteurized	1/8 t. garlic salt
process cheese spread	1 pkg. English muffins, split

Rinse crabmeat in colander and blot dry with paper towels. Mix together remaining ingredients except muffins. Fold in crabmeat, then spread mixture on split muffins. Slice each muffin into 4 wedges. Place on a broiler pan; broil until golden.

Freeze & Serve Instructions: Freeze unbaked English muffins on a baking sheet and freeze; store in freezer bags. To serve, place frozen muffins on a broiler pan. Broil until golden.

Prevent tomato sauce from staining white plastic freezer
containers...easy! Just spray the container with
non-stick vegetable spray before filling.

Helen's Homemade Pasta Sauce   *Makes 11 quarts*

26 lbs. tomatoes, peeled, cored
   and chopped
3 lbs. onions, chopped
2 hot peppers, chopped
2 green peppers, chopped
8 6-oz. cans tomato paste
1-1/2 c. oil
2 c. sugar

1/2 c. salt
2 T. dried oregano
2 T. dried basil
2 T. fresh parsley, chopped
1/2 T. garlic powder
6 bay leaves
11 1-quart plastic freezer
     containers and lids, sterilized

Working in batches, purée tomatoes in a food processor. Place tomatoes, onions, hot and green peppers in a very large pot. Cook over medium-low heat for one hour, stirring often. Mix in remaining ingredients and continue cooking for 1-1/2 hours, stirring frequently to prevent sticking. Let cool; discard bay leaves. Ladle sauce into freezer containers; add lids and freeze.

Freeze & Serve Instructions: To use, thaw overnight in refrigerator. In a saucepan, simmer over medium heat until hot and bubbly.

Square plastic freezing containers take up less room in your
freezer than round ones. To squeeze in even more,
ladle prepared food into plastic zipping bags, seal and
press flat. When frozen, they'll stack easily.

Creamy Mushroom Sauce

Makes about 8 cups

1/3 c. oil
3 T. butter
1/4 c. all-purpose flour
6 c. sliced mushrooms
3/4 c. onion, finely chopped
3/4 t. dried thyme

1/2 t. salt
1/2 t. pepper
3 c. beef broth
1/3 c. cornstarch
3 c. milk

Combine oil, butter and flour in a large Dutch oven; cook and stir over medium heat until golden. Stir in mushrooms, onion and seasonings; cook until onion is tender. Combine broth and cornstarch; add to mushroom mixture, stirring well. Add milk; stir and cook over low heat until thickened and bubbly. Cook for 2 additional minutes. Use immediately as desired or let cool, divide into 3, one-quart plastic zipping freezer bags in 2-2/3 cup portions and freeze.

Freeze & Serve Instructions: Cool; ladle into freezer containers and freeze. To use, thaw overnight in refrigerator. In a microwave-safe bowl, microwave on medium-low setting for 8 to 12 minutes, until hot, stirring once.

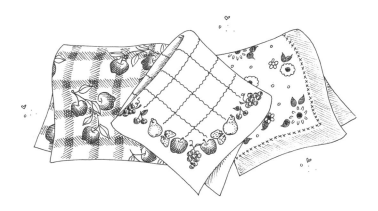

A wide-mouth funnel is handy for filling freezer bags. Stand the open bag in a bowl and hold the bag's top closed around the bottom of the funnel, then just ladle in soup or sauce.

Margaret's Chili Sauce

Makes 5 to 6 pints

16 lbs. tomatoes, peeled
   and chopped
1 onion, chopped
1 green pepper, chopped
1/2 c. cider vinegar
1 c. brown sugar, packed

1 c. sugar
2 t. allspice
2 t. cinnamon
salt and pepper to taste
5 to 6 1-pint plastic freezer
   containers and lids, sterilized

Place tomatoes, onion and green pepper in a large Dutch oven. Add vinegar, sugars and spices; bring to a boil over medium-high heat. Reduce heat to a low simmer. Cook for 1-1/2 to 2 hours, stirring often, until cooked down and thickened. Add salt and pepper to taste. Remove from heat; cool slightly and spoon into containers. Add lids and freeze.

Freeze & Serve Instructions: To use, thaw overnight in refrigerator. In a saucepan, simmer over medium heat until hot and bubbly.

Make a double batch of pesto and freeze some in an ice cube
tray; then seal the cubes in a plastic freezer bag until
you need them for pasta, bread and chicken dishes.

Fresh Herb Pesto Sauce

Makes about 1-1/2 cups

2 c. fresh basil leaves, coarsely
    chopped
6 cloves garlic, chopped
1 c. chopped walnuts or
    pine nuts

1/2 c. plus 1 T. olive oil, divided
1/2 t. salt
3/4 c. grated Parmesan or
    Romano cheese

Mix herbs, garlic, nuts, 1/2 cup oil and salt in a blender. Process
until smooth, adding a little more oil if needed to make blending easier.
Transfer to a bowl and stir in grated cheese. Refrigerate in an airtight
container.

Freeze & Serve Instructions: Spoon into freezer containers or ice cube
trays; freeze. To use, thaw in refrigerator for several hours. Individual
frozen cubes may be added directly to hot liquid.

Post a list of freezer meals right on the fridge and cross them off as they're served. You'll always know what's on the menu for tonight.

Lisa's Chicken Tortilla Soup

Makes 6 to 8 servings

4 14-1/2 oz. cans chicken broth
4 10-oz. cans diced tomatoes
   with chiles
1 c. canned or frozen corn
30-oz. can refried beans

5 c. cooked chicken, shredded
Garnish: shredded Mexican-blend
   or Monterey Jack cheese, corn
   chips or tortilla strips

In a large stockpot over medium heat, combine broth and tomatoes with chiles. Stir in corn and beans; bring to a boil. Reduce heat to low and simmer for 5 to 10 minutes, stirring frequently. Add chicken and heat through. To serve, garnish as desired.

Freeze & Serve Instructions: Cool; do not garnish. Ladle into a freezer container and freeze. Thaw overnight in refrigerator. In a saucepan, simmer over medium heat until hot and bubbly. Garnish as desired.

Wrap up leftover dinner rolls and freeze, then grate while still frozen to use in any recipe that calls for bread crumbs.

Chicken Chili

Serves 6 to 8

2 T. oil
3 boneless, skinless chicken
   breasts, cubed
1 c. onion, chopped
1 c. green pepper, chopped
1/4 t. garlic powder
2 15-oz. cans stewed tomatoes
15-oz. can pinto beans, drained
   and rinsed

3/4 c. picante sauce
1 t. chili powder
1 t. ground cumin
1/2 t. salt
Garnish: shredded Cheddar
   cheese, sour cream,
   chopped avocado

Heat oil in a large pot over medium-high heat; add next 5 ingredients.
Cook until chicken is no longer pink and vegetables are tender. Add
remaining ingredients except garnish; bring to a boil. Reduce heat and
simmer for 20 minutes. Top with cheese, sour cream and avocado.

Freeze & Serve Instructions: Cool; do not garnish. Ladle into a freezer
container and freeze. Thaw overnight in refrigerator. In a saucepan,
simmer over medium heat until hot and bubbly. Garnish as desired.

Fix a double batch! Brown two pounds of ground beef
with two packages of taco seasoning mix, then freeze
half of the mixture for a quick meal of tacos another night.

Mexican 3-Bean Soup

Serves 8 to 10

1 lb. ground beef
1 onion, diced
2 15-1/2 oz. cans kidney beans
2 16-oz. cans pinto beans
2 15-1/2 oz. cans navy beans
15-oz. can corn

14-1/2 oz. can stewed tomatoes
14-1/2 oz. can tomatoes with
  chiles
1-1/4 oz. pkg. taco seasoning mix
1-oz. pkg. ranch salad dressing
  mix

Brown beef and onion over medium heat in a Dutch oven; drain. Add undrained vegetables and seasoning mixes. Simmer, covered, over low heat for one hour.

Freeze & Serve Instructions: Cool; ladle into freezer containers and freeze. Thaw overnight in refrigerator. In a saucepan, simmer over medium heat until hot and bubbly.

Soups freeze well...go ahead and make a double batch,
then freeze half in single-serving containers to enjoy later.
What a time-saver on a busy Saturday!

Italian Vegetable Soup

Makes 8 servings

2 12-oz. pkgs. smoked pork
      sausage, sliced
26-oz. jar spaghetti sauce
2 14-oz. cans chicken broth

2 16-oz. pkgs. frozen Italian
      mixed vegetables
1 onion, diced
6 to 8 c. water

Combine all ingredients in a soup pot. Simmer over medium heat for
20 minutes, or until heated through.

Freeze & Serve Instructions: Cool; ladle into a freezer container and
freeze. Thaw overnight in refrigerator. In a saucepan, simmer over
medium heat until hot and bubbly.

Freeze up chili in small containers...pop in the microwave for
taco salads, chili dogs or nachos at a moment's notice.

Kathi's Chili

Makes 6 servings

1-1/2 lbs. ground beef sirloin
1 yellow onion, diced
1/2 c. green pepper, diced
15-1/2 oz. can dark red kidney
    beans, drained and rinsed
15-1/2 oz. can light red kidney
    beans, drained and rinsed

28-oz. can diced tomatoes
1-1/4 oz. pkg. mild chili
    seasoning mix
1-1/4 oz. pkg. hot chili seasoning
    mix

Brown ground beef in a Dutch oven; drain. Add onion and green pepper; sauté until vegetables are tender. Stir in beans, tomatoes and seasoning mixes. Simmer over medium heat for 10 minutes.

Freeze & Serve Instructions: Cool; ladle into a freezer container and freeze. Thaw overnight in refrigerator. In a saucepan, simmer over medium heat until hot and bubbly.

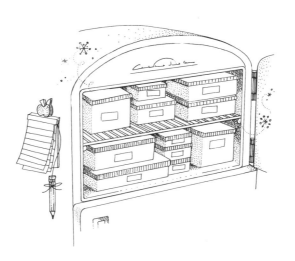

Invite a few friends over and can or freeze summer's bounty
assembly-line style...everyone will go home with
tasty goodies to fill their pantry.

Cucumber Freezer Salad

Makes 6 to 8 servings

2 c. sugar
1 c. cider vinegar
1 t. salt
1 t. celery seed
7 c. cucumbers, peeled and sliced
1 green pepper, sliced

1 red pepper, sliced
3 onions, sliced and separated
    into rings
4 1-quart plastic freezer
    containers and lids, sterilized

In a saucepan, whisk together sugar, vinegar, salt and celery seed. Bring to a boil; boil for one minute. Let cool; set aside. In a large bowl, combine remaining ingredients; pour cooled liquid over top. Toss to coat; divide among freezer containers. Add lids; freeze.

Freeze & Serve Instructions: Store in freezer. To serve, thaw for one to 2 hours in refrigerator.

Fresh garden vegetables make the best broth and it's
so easy! Just add chopped carrots or cabbage to a pot of
boiling water and simmer 30 minutes. Cool, then freeze
in ice cube trays until ready to use.

Freezer Slaw

Makes 6 to 8 servings

1 head cabbage, shredded
1 green pepper, shredded
1 red pepper, shredded

1 carrot, shredded
1-quart plastic freezer container
  and lid, sterilized

In a large bowl, mix all ingredients well. Let stand for one hour. Pour Dressing over slaw. Mix well; place in container. Add lid; freeze.

Dressing:
1/2 c. vinegar
1/2 c. water
2 c. sugar

2 t. salt
1 t. celery seed

Mix all ingredients together; boil for one minute. Cool completely.

Freeze & Serve Instructions: Store in freezer. To serve, thaw in refrigerator for several hours to overnight.

No-fuss thawing...simply move frozen dishes
to the fridge early the day before.

Parsley Baked Rice

Serves 6

3/4 c. long-cooking rice,
    uncooked
1/2 c. butter, sliced
1-1/2 c. boiling water
2 cubes chicken bouillon

1 to 2 T. dried, minced onion
1 t. dried parsley
1 t. celery seed
1/4 t. salt

Mix all ingredients together; stir until butter is slightly melted. Pour into a 2-quart casserole dish that has been sprayed with non-stick vegetable spray. Cover with aluminum foil. Bake at 350 degrees for 30 minutes. Toss with a fork before serving.

Freeze & Serve Instructions: Bake as directed; cool and freeze. Thaw overnight in refrigerator. Bake, covered, at 350 degrees for 15 to 20 minutes, until heated through.

Freeze summer vegetables to enjoy year 'round.
Create a "stew bag" by combining corn, carrots, celery,
onion, broccoli, tomatoes and potatoes for hearty
winter stews and soups.

Iowa Freezer Corn

Makes 10 pints

16 c. corn, sliced from about
    30 ears corn
4 c. water
1 c. sugar

1 T. salt
10 1-pint plastic freezer
    containers and lids, sterilized

Combine all ingredients in a stockpot; stir well. Bring to a boil over medium-high heat. Boil 10 minutes, stirring frequently to keep from sticking or scorching. Ladle into shallow pans to cool; do not drain. Pack corn and liquid in freezer containers; freeze.

Freeze & Serve Instructions: Store in freezer. To serve, simmer frozen corn with a little water until tender.

Quick & easy to make, freezer jams and pickles will
stay fresh for one year. If you choose to
refrigerate them, use within three weeks.

Old-Time Freezer Pickles

Makes 5 to 6 pints

8 c. cucumbers, peeled and thinly
 sliced
2 onions, thinly sliced
2 T. salt

1 c. cider vinegar
1-1/2 c. sugar
5 to 6 1-pint plastic freezer
 containers and lids, sterilized

Combine cucumbers, onions and salt; toss to mix. Cover and refrigerate overnight. Drain; rinse well. Combine vinegar and sugar in a separate bowl. Add to cucumber mixture; mix well. Spoon into freezer containers; add lids and freeze.

Freeze & Serve Instructions: Store in freezer. To serve, thaw in refrigerator for 2 hours to overnight.

Keep a couple of favorite side dishes tucked away in the
freezer for busy days. Pair with hot sandwiches or a
deli roast chicken to put a hearty meal on the table in a hurry.

Freezer Taco Rice

Makes 12 to 18 servings

3 lbs. ground beef, turkey or
   chicken
3 c. onions, diced
3 1-1/4 oz. pkgs. taco seasoning
   mix

6 c. cooked white or brown rice
3 16-oz. cans diced tomatoes
3 8-oz. pkgs. shredded Mexican-
   blend cheese

Brown meat in a large saucepan over medium heat; drain. Add
onion, seasoning mix, rice and tomatoes; simmer until thickened, about
30 minutes. Stir in cheese; cool completely. Package in freezer-safe
containers; freeze.

Freeze & Serve Instructions: Store in freezer. To use, thaw overnight in
refrigerator. Reheat in a saucepan over medium heat and use as desired.

Cut baked lasagna into serving portions and freeze on
a baking sheet, then pack frozen portions in a freezer bag.
Later you can heat up just what you need.

3-Cheese Lasagna

Serves 8

8-oz. can tomato paste
2 16-oz. cans tomato sauce
2 c. water
1/4 c. oil
1-1/2 t. garlic powder
1/8 t. salt
1 t. pepper

15-oz. container ricotta cheese
2 eggs, beaten
3 T. sugar
20 lasagna noodles, cooked
2 c. shredded mozzarella cheese,
    divided
1 c. grated Parmesan cheese

Combine tomato paste, sauce, water, oil and seasonings in a saucepan; bring to a boil. Reduce heat; simmer for 30 minutes. Mix ricotta cheese, eggs and sugar together in a bowl; set aside. In an ungreased 13"x9" baking pan, layer half the sauce mixture, half the noodles, half the ricotta cheese mixture and half the mozzarella cheese; repeat layers. Sprinkle Parmesan cheese on top. Bake, uncovered, at 350 degrees for 45 minutes.

Freeze & Serve Instructions: Prepare as directed; do not bake. Cover with aluminum foil and freeze. To serve, thaw overnight in refrigerator. Follow baking instructions.

Brrr...don't let delicious frozen foods get freezer burn.
Open the freezer door as little as possible to keep
warm air out and fresh taste in.

Baked Chicken Chimies

Makes 6 servings

1-1/2 c. cooked chicken, diced
1-1/3 c. shredded Cheddar cheese
1 c. Southwest bean and corn
   picante salsa
1 t. ground cumin
1/2 t. dried oregano

6 10-inch flour tortillas
2 T. butter, melted
Garnish: shredded Cheddar
   cheese, chopped green onion,
   sour cream, salsa

Mix chicken, cheese, salsa and seasonings together. Spoon about 1/2 cup of mixture in the center of each tortilla. Fold opposite sides over, then roll from the bottom up. Place tortillas seam-side down on a lightly greased baking sheet. Brush with melted butter. Bake, uncovered, for 25 minutes, until golden. Garnish as desired.

Freeze & Serve Instructions: Place unbaked chimies in a freezer container; freeze. To serve, thaw overnight in refrigerator. Place on a baking sheet; bake as directed. Garnish as desired.

Stock up at supermarket sales on large packages of ground beef, chuck steak, chicken or pork chops, then repackage into recipe-size portions before freezing.

Becky's BBQ Beef for a Crowd
Makes 10 to 12 servings

5 to 6-lb. beef chuck roast
salt and pepper to taste
2 14-1/2 oz. cans stewed or
    crushed tomatoes
2 onions, chopped

3 T. sugar
2 T. smoke-flavored cooking
    sauce
Optional: cider vinegar to taste

Place roast in an ungreased large roasting pan; sprinkle with salt and pepper to taste. Mix remaining ingredients. If mixture is too sweet, add vinegar, about one teaspoon at a time. Pour over roast. Cover and bake at 325 degrees for 4 hours, basting occasionally.

Freeze & Serve Instructions: Cool; ladle into freezer containers and freeze. To serve, thaw overnight in refrigerator. In a large saucepan; simmer over medium heat until hot and bubbly.

Don't tie up your casserole dish in the freezer. Line it
with aluminum foil, bake a casserole, wrap and freeze...lift out
the frozen casserole and return to the freezer. To serve,
slip it back into the same dish and bake.

Homesteader's Casserole

Makes 4 to 6 servings

9-oz. pkg. frozen green beans, thawed

8-oz. can small whole onions, drained

1 T. chopped pimentos

1 lb. pork sausage links, browned and drained

3 c. mashed potatoes

8-oz. pkg. pasteurized process cheese spread, sliced

In a large bowl, combine beans, onions and pimentos. Layer half of the sausage, half of the potatoes and half of the cheese in a 2-quart casserole dish coated with non-stick vegetable spray. Layer on remaining potatoes, green bean mixture, remaining sausage and cheese. Bake, covered, at 350 degrees for 30 minutes.

Freeze & Serve Instructions: Cover unbaked casserole tightly with aluminum foil; freeze. To serve, thaw overnight in refrigerator. Uncover; bake as directed.

A quick & easy seasoning mix is six parts salt to one part pepper.
Keep it handy in a large shaker close to the stove.

Cheesy Chicken Chalupas

Makes 10 to 12 servings

2 10-3/4 oz. cans cream of
    chicken soup
16-oz. container sour cream
4-oz. can diced green chiles
2-1/4 oz. can chopped black
    olives, drained
3 green onions, chopped

1 onion, chopped
3 c. shredded Cheddar cheese
4 to 5 chicken breasts, cooked
    and diced
10 to 12 10-inch flour tortillas
2 c. shredded Monterey Jack
    cheese

Mix together soup, sour cream, vegetables and Cheddar cheese in a large bowl. Set aside 1-1/2 cups of soup mixture for topping; add chicken to remaining mixture. Spoon chicken mixture into tortillas; roll up and place into a 13"x9" baking pan coated with non-stick vegetable spray. Spoon reserved soup mixture over tortillas; sprinkle with Monterey Jack cheese. Bake, covered, at 350 degrees for one hour.

Freeze & Serve Instructions: Prepare as directed; do not add cheese. Cover unbaked casserole tightly with aluminum foil; freeze. To serve, thaw overnight in refrigerator. Uncover; sprinkle with cheese and bake as directed.

If a casserole recipe serves too many for your family,
divide ingredients into two smaller dishes, bake and freeze one
for later. It's great to have a heat-and-eat meal
ready when time is short.

Meat & Potato Pie

Makes 4 to 6 servings

1/2 lb. ground beef	14-oz. can sauerkraut, drained
1/2 lb. ground turkey	4 c. mashed potatoes
1/2 onion, chopped	2 c. shredded Swiss cheese

Brown beef, turkey and onion together in a large skillet over medium heat. Place mixture into an ungreased 13"x9" baking dish. Cover beef mixture with sauerkraut; top with mashed potatoes. Bake, uncovered, at 350 degrees for 30 to 35 minutes until potatoes are golden. Top with cheese and bake an additional 5 minutes, or until cheese is melted.

Freeze & Serve Instructions: Top with potatoes; cover unbaked casserole tightly with aluminum foil and freeze. To serve, thaw overnight in refrigerator. Uncover; bake as directed, adding cheese as final step.

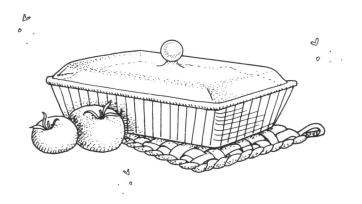

Did you know you can freeze casseroles baked or unbaked?
Let the surface freeze first, then wrap the entire pan with
plastic wrap or aluminum foil. Don't forget to add
extra cooking time to the directions.

Johnny Marzetti

Serves 4

1 lb. ground beef
1 onion, chopped
4-oz. can sliced mushrooms,
    drained
1/8 t. garlic salt
pepper to taste
1-1/2 T. sugar

2 15-oz. cans tomato sauce
1 T. Worcestershire sauce
8-oz. pkg. wide egg noodles,
    cooked and divided
8-oz. pkg. shredded sharp
    Cheddar cheese

Cook ground beef, onion and mushrooms in a large skillet over medium heat; drain. Stir in garlic salt, pepper, sugar and sauces; simmer over low heat for 30 minutes. Layer half the noodles in a greased 2-quart casserole dish. Follow with a layer each of sauce and shredded cheese. Repeat layers. Bake, uncovered, at 375 degrees for 20 to 30 minutes.

Freeze & Serve Instructions: Cover unbaked casserole tightly with aluminum foil; freeze. To serve, thaw overnight in refrigerator. Uncover; bake as directed.

Extra ground beef is tasty in so many easy recipes...tacos,
chili and casseroles to name a few! Brown three or four pounds
at a time, divide it into plastic zipping bags and refrigerate
or freeze for future use.

James' Sloppy Joes

2 lbs. ground beef
1 onion, chopped
1/2 c. green pepper, chopped
1/2 c. celery, chopped
2 14-1/2 oz. cans stewed
    tomatoes
2 c. tomato sauce

1/2 c. catsup
1/4 c. brown sugar, packed
1 T. Worcestershire sauce
1/4 t. salt
1/4 t. pepper
6 to 8 sandwich buns, split

Brown ground beef, onion, green pepper and celery in a large skillet over medium heat; drain. Add remaining ingredients except buns. Bring to a boil; reduce heat and simmer for one hour, stirring occasionally. Spoon onto buns to serve.

Freeze & Serve Instructions: Cool ground beef mixture. Ladle into freezer containers; freeze. To serve, thaw overnight in refrigerator. In a saucepan, simmer over medium heat until hot and bubbly. Spoon onto buns.

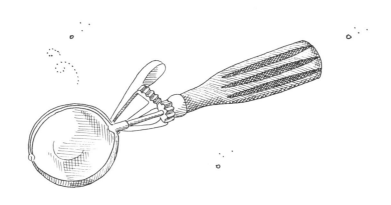

Serve up some "fried" ice cream with a Mexican feast. Freeze scoops of ice cream, roll in crushed frosted corn flake cereal and drizzle with honey. Top with cinnamon, whipped cream and a cherry. Yum!

Teeny's Mexican Casserole

Serves 4 to 6

1 to 1-1/2 lbs. ground beef
1/2 c. onion, chopped
4-oz. can chopped green chiles
3/4 t. salt-free herb seasoning
3/4 t. garlic powder
3/4 t. ground cumin
3/4 t. paprika
salt and pepper to taste

12 6-inch corn tortillas, torn into
   bite-size pieces
10-3/4 oz. can cream of celery or
   mushroom soup
1/4 c. milk
12-oz. pkg. shredded sharp or
   mild Cheddar cheese, divided

Cook ground beef and onion in a skillet until beef is browned and onion is tender. Drain; stir in chiles and seasonings. Place tortilla pieces in a large bowl; add soup, milk and 2 cups cheese. Spoon warm beef mixture over tortillas. Mix all very well and place in a greased 11"x7" baking pan; top with remaining cheese. Bake, uncovered, at 350 degrees for 20 to 25 minutes, until bubbly and golden on top.

Freeze & Serve Instructions: Cover unbaked casserole tightly with aluminum foil; freeze. To serve, thaw overnight in refrigerator. Uncover; bake as directed.

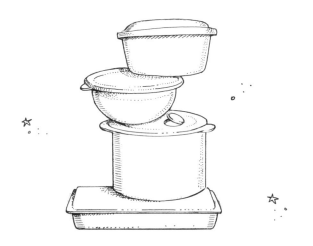

Tasty casserole dishes are ideal for a new mom.
Make several and deliver them to her before the baby
arrives. She can freeze them now, then simply pop dinner
in the oven to bake while baby naps.

Chicken Noodle Bake

Serves 6 to 8

12-oz. pkg. wide egg noodles, cooked
12-oz. pkg. pasteurized process cheese spread, melted
2 boneless, skinless chicken breasts, cooked and cubed

2 10-3/4 oz. cans cream of chicken soup
1 c. chicken broth
1 c. dry bread crumbs
1/4 c. plus 2 T. butter, melted

Combine all ingredients except bread crumbs and butter in a large bowl. Mix well; pour into a greased 13"x9" baking pan and set aside. Combine bread crumbs and butter; mix well to coat and sprinkle over chicken mixture. Bake, uncovered, at 350 degrees for 30 to 40 minutes.

Freeze & Serve Instructions: Cover unbaked casserole tightly with aluminum foil; freeze. To serve, thaw overnight in refrigerator. Uncover; bake as directed.

Don't pass up delicious-sounding recipes that make enough
to serve a farmhouse family when you only need to
serve two. Freeze leftovers for a heat-and-serve
meal later when time is short.

County Fair Maidrites

Makes 20 to 25 servings

5 lbs. ground beef
1/2 c. onion, diced
2 T. salt
2 t. pepper
5 c. catsup
1/3 c. mustard

1/4 c. quick-cooking oats,
    uncooked
3 T. brown sugar, packed
2-1/2 t. Worcestershire sauce
20 to 25 hamburger buns, split

Brown ground beef in a large skillet over medium heat; drain. Add onion, salt and pepper; cook until onion is translucent. Add remaining ingredients except buns; stir and simmer until heated through. Spoon onto buns.

Freeze & Serve Instructions: Cool ground beef mixture. Ladle into freezer containers; freeze. To serve thaw overnight in refrigerator. In a saucepan, simmer over medium heat until hot and bubbly. Spoon onto buns.

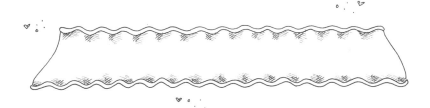

When preparing lasagna for the freezer, be sure to use regular lasagna, not the no-boil kind.

Freeze & Bake Lasagna

28-oz. jar spaghetti sauce
1 lb. ground beef, browned
8-oz. jar mushroom pieces,
    drained
16-oz. container ricotta cheese
1 egg, beaten

1 T. Italian seasoning
8 lasagna noodles, uncooked
    and divided
2 c. shredded Monterey Jack
    cheese
2 c. shredded mozzarella cheese

Combine sauce, beef and mushrooms; set aside. Mix ricotta cheese, egg and Italian seasoning together; set aside. Layer as follows in each of 2 ungreased 9"x5" loaf pans: one cup meat sauce, 2 lasagna noodles, 1/2 cup ricotta cheese mixture, 1/2 cup Monterey Jack cheese and 1/2 cup mozzarella cheese. Repeat layers. Cover with aluminum foil; bake at 350 degrees for 1-1/2 hours.

Freeze & Serve Instructions: Prepare as directed; do not bake. Cover with aluminum foil; freeze. To serve, thaw overnight in refrigerator. Bake as directed.

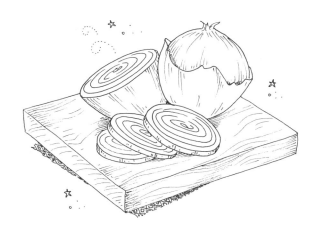

When chopping onions or celery, it only takes a moment to chop a little extra. Tuck them away in the freezer for a quick start to dinner another day.

Colorado Ham & Cheese

Makes 16 servings

1/2 lb. cooked ham, shredded
1/2 lb. shredded sharp Cheddar
   cheese
2 eggs, hard-boiled, peeled and
   finely chopped
1/2 c. onion, finely chopped

1/2 c. green olives with pimentos,
   finely chopped
1/2 c. chili sauce
3 T. mayonnaise
16 hot dog buns, split

Combine first 5 ingredients; set aside. Mix together chili sauce and
mayonnaise; add to ham mixture. Spoon into buns and wrap
individually in aluminum foil. Bake at 375 degrees for 15 minutes,
or until heated through.

Freeze & Serve Instructions: Freeze wrapped, unbaked buns. To serve,
thaw desired number of buns for 2 to 3 hours in the refrigerator. Bake
as directed.

Need to cool dinner down quickly to freeze for later? Divide
it into individual servings first and refrigerate. Freezing
single-size entrées makes dinner a breeze... just
thaw and reheat!

Quick Skillet Spaghetti

Serves 4 to 6

1 lb. sweet Italian ground pork
   sausage
1 clove garlic, pressed
7-oz. pkg. spaghetti, uncooked
   and broken into 1-inch
   lengths

15-oz. can tomato sauce
2 14-oz. cans diced Italian
   tomatoes
1 T. fresh parsley, chopped
2 t. dried basil
3 T. shredded Italian-blend cheese

In a skillet over medium heat, brown sausage for 5 to 7 minutes, stirring often. Drain; stir in garlic and broken spaghetti. Cook for 5 minutes, stirring often. Add remaining ingredients except cheese and stir until well blended. Heat to boiling. Reduce heat to low; cover and simmer about 20 minutes, until spaghetti is tender. Sprinkle with cheese. Cover and cook for 2 to 3 minutes longer to melt cheese.

Freeze & Serve Instructions: Prepare as directed, omitting cheese; cool. Package in a freezer bag; freeze. To serve, thaw overnight in refrigerator. In a skillet, cover and simmer over medium-low heat until hot. Add cheese.

Freeze homemade mashed potatoes in individual muffin cups.
Once they're frozen, pop them out, store in plastic
freezer bags and microwave as needed.

Spicy Fried Chicken

2 c. all-purpose flour
2 T. Cajun seasoning
1-1/2 t. garlic powder
1-1/2 t. onion powder
1 T. salt

1-1/2 t. pepper
4 eggs, beaten
1/4 to 1/2 c. milk
6 lbs. chicken
oil for frying

Combine flour and seasonings in a large plastic zipping bag; set aside. Whisk together eggs and milk. Shake chicken in flour mixture, then dip in egg mixture. Heat 1/4 inch oil in a large skillet over medium heat. Fry chicken until golden. Reduce heat and cook until juices run clear, turning several times, about 30 minutes.

Freeze & Serve Instructions: Fry chicken; cool. Wrap in serving-size packages in aluminum foil; freeze. To serve, thaw at room temperature one hour before baking. Open up wrapping; place package on oven rack. Bake at 375 degrees for 45 minutes, until heated through.

Up to two days before serving, put a frozen casserole in the fridge to thaw slightly. When ready to serve, cover with aluminum foil and bake at 350 degrees for one hour. Remove foil and bake 30 minutes more, or until heated through.

Pizza Casserole

Makes 16 to 20 servings

2 lbs. ground beef
1 onion, chopped
2 28-oz. jars spaghetti sauce
16-oz. pkg. spiral pasta, cooked

2 8-oz. pkgs. shredded
    mozzarella cheese
8-oz. pkg. sliced pepperoni

In a large skillet over medium heat, brown beef and onion; drain. Stir
in spaghetti sauce and pasta. Transfer to 2 greased 13"x9" baking pans.
Sprinkle with cheese; top with pepperoni. Bake, uncovered, at
350 degrees for 25 to 30 minutes.

Freeze & Serve Instructions: Prepare casseroles, but do not add cheese
and pepperoni. Cover unbaked casseroles tightly with aluminum foil;
freeze. To serve, thaw overnight in refrigerator. Uncover; top with cheese
and pepperoni. Bake as directed.

Freezer tip...never buy frozen food that's covered with frost. It has probably been defrosted and refrozen.

Easy Cheesy Enchiladas

Serves 12 to 16

3 lbs. ground beef
2 1-1/4 oz. pkgs. taco seasoning
   mix
1 to 1-1/2 c. water
16-oz. can refried beans
2 pkgs. 10-inch flour tortillas
10-3/4 oz. can cream of
   mushroom soup

10-3/4 oz. can cream of chicken
   soup
2 10-oz. cans tomatoes with
   chiles
1-1/2 lbs. pasteurized process
   cheese spread, cubed

Brown ground beef in a large skillet over medium heat; drain. Add seasoning mix and water; simmer for 5 minutes. Add beans; cook for an additional 5 minutes. Spread mixture down center of tortillas; roll up. Arrange seam-side down in 2 greased 13"x9" baking pans; set aside. Cook remaining ingredients in a saucepan over medium heat until cheese is melted; spoon over enchiladas. Bake at 350 degrees for 15 minutes, until bubbly.

Freeze & Serve Instructions: Cover unbaked casseroles tightly with aluminum foil; freeze. To serve, thaw overnight in refrigerator. Uncover and bake as directed, covering again if top begins to brown.

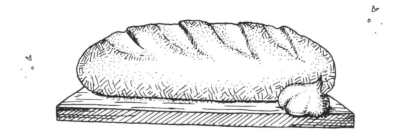

Buy loaves of savory bread at the market and then
freeze them. They will keep well and for dinner,
just thaw and toast.

Broccoli Chicken & Rice

Serves 4

2 c. cooked chicken, chopped
10-oz. pkg. frozen broccoli,
    thawed
1 c. carrot, peeled and sliced
1/2 c. onion, chopped
3 T. lemon juice
2 T. margarine
1 T. cornstarch

2 cubes chicken bouillon
4 t. dried parsley
1 t. lemon zest
1/2 t. salt
1/2 t. garlic, minced
1 c. long-cooking rice, uncooked
2 c. water

In a bowl, combine all ingredients except rice and water; mix well. Spoon into a large saucepan. Bring to a boil over medium heat; add rice and water. Simmer, covered, over low heat for 20 minutes, or until rice is tender. If frozen, to serve, thaw overnight in refrigerator. Follow cooking directions above.

Freeze & Serve Instructions: Before adding rice and water, spoon into a freezer container; freeze. To serve, thaw overnight in refrigerator. In a large saucepan, cook as directed, adding rice and water at this time.

Freezing cooked rice makes for quick-fix meals later. Use it
for stir-fry dishes, to make soups thick & hearty or mix in
fresh vegetables for an easy side dish...just freeze
servings flat in plastic zipping bags.

Honey-Pepper Pork

Serves 4

1-1/2 lbs. boneless pork loin,
    cubed
2 T. oil
.75-oz. pkg. brown gravy mix
1 c. water
1/4 c. honey
3 T. soy sauce

2 T. red wine vinegar
1/2 t. ground ginger
1/8 t. garlic powder
1 green pepper, chopped
1 red pepper, chopped
1 onion, chopped

In a large skillet over medium heat, sauté pork in oil until browned, about 15 minutes; drain. Add gravy mix, water, honey, soy sauce, vinegar, ginger and garlic powder; stir well. Cover and reduce heat to low; simmer for 15 minutes, until sauce thickens. Add peppers and onion; simmer until vegetables are tender.

Freeze & Serve Instructions: After adding peppers and onion, cool. Package in a freezer bag; freeze. To serve, thaw overnight in refrigerator. In a saucepan, cover and simmer over medium heat until heated through and vegetables are tender.

Put a few extra burgers on the grill, then pop into buns,
wrap individually and freeze. Later, just reheat in the
microwave for quick meals...they'll taste freshly grilled!

Donna's Juicy Burgers

Serves 8

2 lbs. ground beef
1 c. Italian-seasoned dry bread
   crumbs
1 onion, chopped
2 to 3 cloves garlic, minced

2 eggs, beaten
1/2 to 1 t. salt
1/8 t. pepper
8 sandwich buns, split

Combine together all ingredients except buns; mix well. Form into 8 patties. Grill burgers over medium heat to desired doneness. Serve on buns.

Freeze & Serve Instructions: Cool burgers; wrap individually in plastic wrap. To serve, unwrap; place on a microwave-safe plate and microwave for 2 to 4 minutes, until heated through. Serve on buns.

Oops, the family's dinner plans have changed, and dinner is already thawing. No problem! As long as some ice crystals remain, it's perfectly safe to return partially defrosted food to the freezer.

Gardeners' Casserole

Serves 8

1 head cauliflower, chopped
1 bunch broccoli, chopped
8 carrots, peeled and sliced
   1-inch thick
1 t. fresh chives, minced
salt and pepper to taste
1 onion, chopped

1/2 c. butter
1/4 c. all-purpose flour
8-oz. container whipping cream
2 c. milk
8-oz. pkg. cream cheese, softened
1 c. shredded Cheddar cheese
1 c. seasoned croutons, crushed

Steam cauliflower, broccoli and carrots until crisp-tender. Place vegetables in a lightly greased 13"x9" baking pan; sprinkle with chives, salt and pepper. Set aside. In a saucepan over medium heat, sauté onion in butter; gradually add flour, stirring constantly. Stir in cream and milk; add cream cheese, stirring constantly, until thick and smooth. Pour cheese sauce over vegetables and mix gently. Sprinkle with cheese and croutons. Bake, uncovered, at 325 degrees for 30 to 35 minutes.

Freeze & Serve Instructions: Prepare casserole but omit cheese and crouton topping. Cover unbaked casserole tightly with aluminum foil; freeze. To serve, thaw overnight in refrigerator. Uncover; top with cheese and croutons. Bake as directed.

To freeze a just-made casserole, let it stand at
room temperature for 30 minutes, then refrigerate for
30 minutes more. When cool, wrap it tightly with aluminum foil;
label and freeze up to 3 months.

Lazy Pierogie

15 lasagna noodles, cooked
   and divided
2 c. mashed potatoes
2 eggs, beaten
8-oz. pkg. shredded Cheddar
   cheese

garlic salt, pepper and onion
   powder to taste
1/2 c. butter
1 onion, chopped
Garnish: sour cream

Arrange 5 lasagna noodles in a lightly greased 13"x9" baking pan; set aside. Combine potatoes, eggs, cheese and seasonings; spread half of mixture over lasagna. Cover with another 5 lasagna noodles; spread with remaining potato mixture. Top with remaining lasagna noodles; set aside. Melt butter in a skillet over medium heat; sauté onion until tender. Pour onion mixture over lasagna. Cover with aluminum foil; bake at 350 degrees for 30 minutes. Let stand for 10 minutes before slicing into squares. Serve with sour cream on the side.

Freeze & Serve Instructions: Cover unbaked casserole tightly with aluminum foil; freeze. To serve, thaw overnight in refrigerator. Bake and serve as directed.

Team up! Invite a friend over and prepare several casseroles together. Having someone to chat with makes prep time go quickly and when all the work is done, you'll both have casseroles to freeze...a real time-saver.

Carolyn's Chicken Tetrazzini

Serves 8

2 c. sliced mushrooms
1/4 c. butter
3 T. all-purpose flour
2 c. chicken broth
1/4 c. light cream
3 T. sherry or chicken broth
1 T. fresh parsley, chopped

1 t. salt
1/8 t. pepper
1/8 t. nutmeg
3 c. cooked chicken, cubed
8-oz. pkg. spaghetti, cooked
1 c. grated Parmesan cheese

In a Dutch oven over medium heat, sauté mushrooms in butter until tender. Stir in flour. Add chicken broth; cook, stirring constantly, until sauce is thickened. Remove from heat; stir in cream, sherry or broth and seasonings. Fold in chicken and cooked spaghetti; turn mixture into a lightly greased 13"x9" baking pan. Sprinkle with Parmesan cheese. Cover with aluminum foil and bake at 350 degrees for 30 to 35 minutes, until heated through. Let stand for 5 to 10 minutes.

Freeze & Serve Instructions: Cover unbaked casserole tightly with aluminum foil; freeze. To serve, thaw overnight in refrigerator. Uncover; bake as directed.

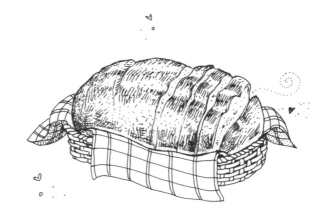

Bakery-fresh bread...easy! Thaw frozen dough,
roll out and sprinkle with minced garlic and chopped rosemary.
Roll up and bake as the package directs.

Polynesian Spareribs

Makes 4 to 6 servings

4 lbs. pork spareribs, cut into
    serving-size portions
2 onions, chopped
2 carrots, peeled and chopped
2 T. oil
1-1/3 c. pineapple juice
2/3 c. red wine vinegar

2 T. Worcestershire sauce
2 t. soy sauce
2/3 c. brown sugar, packed
2 T. cornstarch
1/2 c. water
juice and zest of 1 lemon
salt and pepper to taste

Arrange spareribs in a roasting pan. Bake, uncovered, at 425 degrees for
20 minutes. Drain drippings from pan; set ribs aside. In a saucepan over
medium heat, sauté vegetables in oil until tender. Add pineapple juice,
vinegar, sauces and sugar. Simmer over low heat for 20 minutes, stirring
occasionally. Combine cornstarch and water in a bowl; stir into sauce
along with remaining ingredients. Bring to a boil, stirring constantly.
Reduce heat to low; simmer until thickened. Pour sauce over ribs. Bake
at 350 degrees for 40 minutes, basting every 10 minutes.

Freeze & Serve Instructions: Bake as directed; cool. Wrap in aluminum
foil; freeze. To serve, thaw overnight in refrigerator. Place in roasting
pan; cover and bake at 400 degrees for 30 minutes. Uncover;
bake 15 minutes more.

A speedy side...sauté frozen green beans in a little olive oil until crisp-tender and toss with a jar of roasted red peppers.

Cube Steak in Savory Gravy

Serves 4

1 lb. beef cube steak, cut into
    4 serving-size pieces
1/4 c. all-purpose flour
1 onion, chopped
1 T. oil
1 c. water

1/4 c. catsup
1 T. Worcestershire sauce
1 t. beef bouillon granules
1/2 t. Italian seasoning
1 t. salt
1/4 t. pepper

Coat beef pieces with flour; set aside. In a skillet over medium heat, sauté onion in oil until translucent. Add beef and brown on both sides; drain. Mix remaining ingredients in a small bowl; pour over beef mixture. Heat until boiling; reduce heat. Cover and simmer until beef is tender, about 1-1/4 to 1-1/2 hours.

Freeze & Serve Instructions: Prepare as directed; cool. Place in a freezer container; freeze. To serve, thaw overnight in refrigerator. In a skillet, cover and simmer over low heat until heated through.

Most fruit pies can be frozen up to four months. Cool after
baking, then wrap in plastic wrap and aluminum foil before
freezing. To serve, thaw overnight in the fridge,
bring to room temperature and warm in the oven.

Dreamy Orange Pie

Serves 8 to 10

2 c. gingersnap cookies, crushed
1/4 c. chopped pecans
1/4 c. butter, melted
1 qt. orange sherbet, softened

1 to 1-1/2 c. vanilla ice cream,
  softened
8-oz. container frozen whipped
  topping, thawed

Mix together cookie crumbs, pecans and melted butter; press into an ungreased 9" deep-dish pie plate. Spread 1/3 of the sherbet over crust; spread 1/3 of the ice cream over sherbet. Repeat layers; freeze for 2 to 3 hours.

Freeze & Serve Instructions: Store in freezer. To serve, let stand at room temperature for 20 minutes before slicing. Spread whipped topping over top.

Frozen grapes, strawberries and raspberries make flavorful
ice cubes in frosty beverages. Freeze washed and dried
fruit in a plastic zipping bag for up to 3 months...perfect for
all the summer gatherings.

Rainbow Sherbet Cake

Makes 12 to 15 servings

1 prepared angel food cake
1 pt. orange sherbet, softened
1 pt. raspberry sherbet, softened
1 pt. lime sherbet, softened

12-oz. container frozen whipped
  topping, thawed
Garnish: gumdrops

Slice angel food cake crosswise to make 4 equal layers; place bottom layer on serving plate. Spread orange sherbet evenly over the top; repeat with next 2 cake layers using raspberry and lime sherbet. Top with final cake layer; frost with whipped topping. Cover; freeze until firm, about one hour.

Freeze & Serve Instructions: Store in freezer. To serve, let stand at room temperature for a few minutes. Garnish with gumdrops; slice.

When draining canned fruit, freeze the juice in ice cube
trays...oh-so handy for adding a little sweetness
to marinades and dressings.

Creamy Frozen Salad

Makes 4 to 6 servings

2 c. sour cream
2 T. lemon juice
3/4 c. sugar
1 banana, mashed

1/2 t. salt
9-oz. can crushed pineapple
1/4 c. maraschino cherries,
    drained and chopped

Blend sour cream, lemon juice and sugar; add banana. Stir in the remaining ingredients. Pour into a mold or muffin tins for individual servings. Cover with plastic wrap; place in freezer until frozen.

Freeze & Serve Instructions: Store in freezer. To serve, dip mold or muffin tip in warm water to loosen.

On a leisurely day at home, bake up a double batch of cookies and freeze them. Later, your family can enjoy home-baked goodies even when you're on the road...simply thaw and serve!

Rocky Road Frozen Sandwiches

Makes 16

1 c. chocolate frosting
1/2 c. mini marshmallows
32 graham cracker squares,
    divided

1/2 c. marshmallow creme
1/2 gal. chocolate ice cream,
    softened

Mix together frosting and marshmallows; spread over half of graham crackers. Spread marshmallow creme over remaining graham crackers. Spread 1/2 cup ice cream onto each graham cracker coated with frosting mixture. Top with remaining graham crackers. Wrap individually in plastic wrap and freeze until firm.

Freeze & Serve Instructions: Store in freezer. At serving time, let stand at room temperature for a few minutes.

Life is uncertain; eat dessert first!
-Ernestine Ulmer

Grandma & Katie's Frozen Dessert   *Serves 15 to 18*

1/2 c. creamy peanut butter
1/2 c. light corn syrup
2 c. crispy rice cereal
2 c. chocolate-flavored crispy
    rice cereal

1/2 gal. vanilla ice cream,
    softened
1/2 to 1 c. Spanish peanuts
Garnish: chocolate syrup

Blend together peanut butter and corn syrup in a large bowl. Add cereals;
stir until coated. Press into the bottom of a ungreased 13"x9" baking pan.
Spread ice cream over cereal mixture; sprinkle with peanuts. Swirl
chocolate syrup over top. Cover with aluminum foil; freeze at least
4 hours.

Freeze & Serve Instructions: Store in freezer. To serve, let stand at room
temperature for a few minutes; cut into squares.

To freeze fresh berries, coat a cookie sheet with non-stick vegetable spray; spread berries on sheet in a single layer and freeze until solid. Remove from tray and place in plastic freezer bags.

Frozen Raspberry Dessert

Makes 12 to 15 servings

1 c. all-purpose flour
1/2 c. chopped walnuts

1/4 c. brown sugar, packed
1/2 c. margarine, melted

Mix flour, nuts, brown sugar and margarine together. Press into a 2-quart oblong cake pan. Bake at 350 degrees for 15 to 20 minutes. Cool and break into crumbs with a fork. Reserve 1/3 of the crumbs and spread the rest evenly in the pan. Pour Filling over top. Sprinkle reserved crumbs on top. Cover; freeze at least 2 hours.

Filling:
2 pasteurized egg whites
3/4 c. sugar
2 T. lemon juice

2 c. raspberries
8-oz. container frozen whipped
  topping, thawed

Beat egg whites with an electric mixer on high speed until stiff peaks form. Slowly add remaining ingredients. Mix well.

Freeze & Serve Instructions: Store in freezer. To serve, let stand at room temperature for about 15 minutes. Cut into squares.

Make freezer preserves. Combine one pound berries,
1-1/2 cups sugar and 2 tablespoons lemon juice. Bring to a boil,
reduce heat and simmer, uncovered, for 30 minutes. Spoon into
sterilized freezer containers and freeze for up to 6 months.

Emily's Frozen Fruit Salad

Makes 10 to 12 servings

16-oz. can apricot halves
20-oz. can crushed pineapple
10-oz. pkg. frozen strawberries,
    thawed
6-oz. can frozen orange juice
    concentrate, thawed

1/2 c. water
1/2 c. sugar
3 bananas, sliced

Combine undrained apricots and pineapple. Mix in remaining ingredients except bananas; set aside. Arrange bananas in a 13"x9" baking pan; pour fruit mixture over top. Cover and freeze for at least 24 hours.

Freeze & Serve Instructions: Store in freezer. To serve, let stand at room temperature for about 15 minutes. Cut into squares.

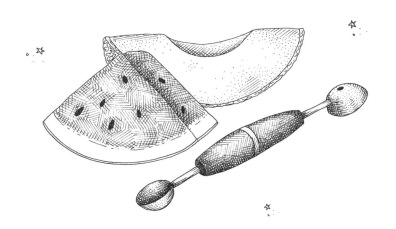

Spoon fruit sherbet into hollowed-out lemons, limes, oranges or melons...they make the prettiest serving "bowls"!

Frozen "Watermelon" Slices

Makes 8 servings

1 honeydew melon
1 gal. raspberry sherbet

Garnish: semi-sweet chocolate
chips

Refrigerate melon for at least 2 hours so that it is well chilled; slice in half. Scoop out seeds; pack each center with raspberry sherbet. Slice each half into 4 wedges; press chocolate chips into the sherbet along the bottom edges to look like seeds. Slice to serve.

Freeze & Serve Instructions: Wrap well with plastic wrap; freeze. To serve, let stand at room temperature for a few minutes before cutting into slices.

Make your own delicious frosty fruit pops...it's easy!
Slice your favorite fruit and combine with fresh juice. Pour into
small cups and set in the freezer. When partially frozen,
insert wooden treat sticks, then freeze until firm.

Apple-Cranberry Pops

Makes 6

12-oz. can unsweetened frozen
   apple-cranberry juice
   concentrate, thawed

2 c. plain yogurt
2 t. vanilla extract

Mix ingredients together; pour into small paper cups. Insert a wooden treat stick into the center of each yogurt cup; freeze overnight.

Freeze & Serve Instructions: Store in freezer. Let stand at room temperature for a few minutes; peel off paper cups.

INDEX

Our Story

Back in 1984, we were next-door neighbors raising our families in the little town of Delaware, Ohio. Two moms with small children, we were looking for a way to do what we loved and stay home with the kids too. We had always shared a love of home cooking and making memories with family & friends and so, after many a conversation over the backyard fence, **Gooseberry Patch** was born.

We put together our first catalog at our kitchen tables, enlisting the help of our loved ones wherever we could. From that very first mailing, we found an immediate connection with many of our customers and it wasn't long before we began receiving letters, photos and recipes from these new friends. In 1992, we put together our very first cookbook, compiled from hundreds of these recipes and, the rest, as they say, is history.

Hard to believe it's been over 35 years since those kitchen-table days! From that original little **Gooseberry Patch** family, we've grown to include an amazing group of creative folks who love cooking, decorating and creating as much as we do. Today, we're best known for our homestyle, family-friendly cookbooks, now recognized as national bestsellers.

One thing's for sure, we couldn't have done it without our friends all across the country. Each year, we're honored to turn thousands of your recipes into our collectible cookbooks. Our hope is that each book captures the stories and heart of all of you who have shared with us. Whether you've been with us since the beginning or are just discovering us, welcome to the **Gooseberry Patch** family!

Visit our website anytime
www.gooseberrypatch.com

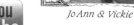

Jo Ann & Vickie

1·800·854·6673